A Little of This and a Little of That

by

Amy Lawrence

Published by:
ATR Publishing

Cover Photo by:
Raggedy Annie Photography
Annie Jornlin
(916)780-6159
Raggedyanniephotography.com

Back Cover Photo by:
Sirlin Photographers
(916)444-8464
http://www.sirlin.com/

ISBN: 978-0-9796170-1-0

An Afternoon to Remember is dedicated to educating others in the art of taking tea. Our mission is to provide a unique upscale experience where customers are pampered and can relax, socialize and celebrate special occasions while enjoying excellent teas and delectable treats. Tea rooms entice you to sit leisurely, and this is the main goal and purpose of our tea room making your experience here truly...

"An Afternoon to Remember."

Forward

The title of this cookbook, "A Little of This and A Little of That", represents the way we at An Afternoon to Remember cook. We are constantly taking bits and pieces from other recipes and cookbooks and combining them to make our own creations. Our measurements are not exact. We cook according to what we like and what we think our customers will like. When you use this cookbook, please remember that and add the amount of ingredients according to your tastes. If you feel that 5 cloves of garlic is too much, then don't use quite that much. For the most part we use fresh herbs, so if it says, 2T. of rosemary, then it means fresh rosemary. If you are using dried herbs, then use less. On the sandwiches, if the sandwich filling is too thick and won't spread, add a little more sour cream to thin it out. Also if the soup seems too thick then add a little more broth. Go with your own instincts. Try adding new ingredients to the recipes to create your own. Above all have fun!

Dedication

I would like to dedicate this cookbook to my family and staff. Without them An Afternoon to Remember would not be possible.

First of all I would like to thank my staff. They are the greatest. Words cannot even begin to express my gratitude and feelings for them. They are so talented. Each of them brings a unique quality to our tea room. Their loyalty and dedication is amazing and can be seen every day. They come in early, stay late, work in the heat, and have even worked without electricity a few times. I can count on them whenever I need them. I can't believe that I even opened the tea room without having them already in place. They have developed and refined the art of serving tea. Our success is due to their talents and efforts.

I would also like to thank my family.

My husband is my rock of strength. He patiently listens to me and guides me. Without him, I would have never had the courage to do this. He never complains of my long hours or lack of energy at times at home. He is my computer guru. He edits my work, gets the newsletters and cookbooks out on time. He can fix just about anything, including my 1940's iron that I

Dedication Continued

use to iron all of the napkins. He even irons the napkins for me when I'm too tired. In addition, he cooks dinner and is a wonderful father.

My boys are the joy of my life. They help me constantly. They often fold tea room laundry, put stamps on newsletters and even help do housework.

My mother is always there for me. She celebrates the successes of my life and listens patiently to all of my woes. When visiting, she brings joy to my customers with her smile and conversation and even when she's back in Missouri, she brings joy with her wonderful tea cozies. Most of all, I would like to thank her for her enthusiasm which encourages me to continue on.

Last I would like to thank my in-laws. They are so patient and understanding when I can't attend all of our family events due to events at the tea room. They are there for me whenever I need them to help out with the boys.

I couldn't have done this without all of these wonderful people. So thanks to them all!

Table of Contents

Table of Contents Continued

Sandwiches

Desserts

Table of Contents Continued

Desserts

Scones

Ideas to Make Your Tea Party More Intimate

Use fresh flowers – try using a tea pot or a tea cup for a vase.

Use decorated sugar-mix white sugar cubes with a few decorated cubes.

Make personalized name cards for each guest.

Have guests bring and wear hats – this breaks down the intimidation of going to a "formal" tea party and everyone has fun.

Fold napkins creatively, try placing a flower on each napkin.

Garnish your tea tray for a gorgeous effect. Try using edible leaves from your garden such as scented geraniums, mint, oregano, basil and savory.

Offer guests several different types of tea, be sure to include a tisane.

Use tea cozies or tea warmers to keep the tea warm.

Have guests bring their own tea cup and a related story about their cup.

Tea

The Perfect Pot of Tea

Fill kettle with freshly drawn cold water.

Temper teapot by filling with hot water.

Bring kettle to boil.

Pour out water in teapot.

Place tea sock in teapot.

Add one scant teaspoon of tea per cup.

Pour boiling water over leaves.

Replace teapot lid.

Steep for 3-5 minutes for black tea.

Decant or remove tea sock with leaves.

Stir and serve.

Cover with a tea cozy or use a warmer to keep tea piping hot.

Enjoy!

Gourmet Iced Tea

To brew one gallon of gourmet iced tea with loose tea leaves:

Use fresh, cold water from the tap or spring water. Do not reuse water you have already boiled since the oxygen will have evaporated and this affects the taste of the tea.

Measure ⅓ cup of tea leaves (to make one gallon) into your infuser. For teas or herbals that require a heaping teaspoon for one cup of tea, like Rooibos, use ½ cup of leaves. For this quantity of leaves, you will need a large infuser for the leaves to have room to expand and brew properly. A cotton tea sock or the large basket infuser will work.

Heat the water until it reaches the correct temperature: generally, steaming for green and almost a full boil for black teas, oolongs, herbal infusions and fruit blends. Pour it over the leaves immediately and cover your teapot.

Brew the tea for 5 minutes for black teas, 2-3 minutes for green and 10 minutes for Rooibos. Over brewing can also cause the tea to taste bitter.

Gourmet Iced Tea Continued

After the brewing, remove the leaves immediately.

Transfer the tea to your pitcher and sweeten if desired. Then, add enough cold tap water to make one gallon.

A 2 ounce tin of loose tea will yield 3 gallons of iced tea and a 4 ounce tin will yield 5-6 gallons of iced tea.

Almond Fruit Tea

- 3 T. loose Assam tea
- 8 cups of boiling water, plus enough cold water to fill a one gallon container
- 2 cups sugar (start with 1 cup and add the rest to taste, this is a very sweet tea)
- 1 12 oz can frozen lemonade
- 4 tsp. almond extract

Place loose tea in a tea sock or strainer. Pour 8 cups of boiling water over the leaves. Steep for 4 minutes. Remove leaves from tea. Mix tea, sugar, lemonade and almond extract in a one gallon container. Fill the rest of the container with water. Serve over ice.

Makes 1 gallon.

Notes

Soups

Baked Potato Soup

- 4 large baking potatoes
- ⅔ c. butter
- ⅔ c. flour
- 6 c. of milk
- ¾ t. salt
- ½ t. pepper
- 4 green onions, chopped and divided
- 2 minced garlic cloves
- 12 slices of bacon, cooked, crumbled and divided
- 1¼ c. cheddar cheese, shredded
- 8 oz. sour cream

Bake potatoes at 400° for one hour; let cool. Cut in half length-wise, and scoop out pulp. Set aside. Discard skins.

Melt butter in a heavy sauce pan over low heat. Add flour. Stir until smooth. Cook one minute, stirring constantly. Gradually add milk. Cook over medium heat, stirring constantly until mixture is thickened and bubbly.

Add potato pulp, salt, pepper, 2 T. green onion, 2 minced garlic cloves, ½ c. crumbled bacon

Notes

Baked Potato Soup
Continued

and 1 c. cheese. Cook until thoroughly heated, then stir in sour cream. Add extra milk, if necessary.

Serve with remaining green onions, bacon and cheese. Makes about 10 cups. Even better if reheated the next day.

Notes

Cream of Asparagus Soup

- 3 lbs. fresh asparagus
- 1 large onion-finely chopped
- 7 cloves of garlic (or to taste) – minced
- ¾ c. butter
- 1 c. flour
- 4 c. chicken stock (we use chicken bouillon to make our stock – provides more intense flavor)
- 7 c. milk
- ½ c. cream
- pepper to taste

Wash and trim asparagus. Cut into 1 inch pieces. Put in glass bowl. Add ½ c. water. Cover with a plate or wrap. Microwave on high until tender 5-10 minutes. Drain. Chop or pulse in food processor-rough chop, not mush.

Saute onions and garlic in butter on low heat for about 45 minutes. Stir occasionally so they do not scorch. Add 1 c. flour. Stir in 4 c. chicken stock. Add 6-7 c. of milk and ½ c. cream. Add cooked asparagus. Add pepper to taste. Add more milk if soup is too thick. Simmer on low for 1 hour. This soup is best if made the day before and reheated. Makes a lot!

Notes

Cream of Spinach Soup

- 2 pkg. frozen spinach
- 1 large onion-finely chopped
- 4-6 cloves of garlic(or to taste) – minced
- ¾ c. butter
- 1 c. flour
- 4 c. chicken stock (we use chicken bouillon to make our stock-provides more intense flavor)
- 7 c. milk
- ½ c. cream
- pepper to taste

Saute onions and garlic in butter on low heat for about 45 minutes. Stir occasionally so they do not scorch. Add 1 c. flour. Stir in 4 c. chicken stock. Add 6-7 c. of milk and ½ c. cream. Add spinach. Add pepper to taste. Add more milk if soup is too thick. Simmer on low for 1 hour. This soup is best if made the day before and reheated. Makes a lot!

Notes

Salad

Orzo Florentine

- 6 c. julienne-shredded fresh spinach
- 3 ripe Roma tomatoes, diced
- ¼ c. pine nuts, lightly toasted
- ¼-½ c. sun-dried tomatoes, julienne cut
- 1 small jar capers
- 1 small can black olives – sliced
- 1 radicchio – cut into strips
- 5 ounces orzo pasta, cooked and chilled
- ¼ c. grated Parmesan
- Fresh cracked pepper, for garnish
- Roasted Garlic Lemon Vinaigrette-recipe follows

Place all ingredients in a chilled mixing bowl. Toss. Add Roasted Garlic Lemon Vinaigrette to taste.

Garnish with shaved Parmesan cheese and fresh cracked pepper.

Notes

Roasted Garlic Lemon Vinaigrette

- ¼ c. red wine vinegar
- 3T. honey
- ½ t. salt
- 5 cloves of roasted garlic
- ¾ c. olive oil
- Juice of ½ lemon or add enough to taste

Place vinegar, honey, salt and roasted garlic in a food processor. Puree until garlic is chopped and very fine. With the food processor still running, add olive oil and lemon juice. Refrigerate until ready to use.

To roast garlic: Trim off the top of 1 bulb. Brush with a little olive oil. Place in foil and bake at 500° for 30 minutes. Remove paper skins and use garlic pulp for recipe.

Notes

Sandwiches

Cheese Puffs

- 1 loaf unsliced white bread
- ¼ lb. butter
- 8 oz. cheddar cheese, grated
- 3 oz. cream cheese, cubed
- 2 stiffly beaten egg whites.

Cut the bread into 1 inch cubes (freeze loaf for a few minutes, cut off crusts)

Melt butter, cream cheese, and cheddar cheese in double boiler. Fold in egg whites. Dip bread cubes into mixture. Refrigerate on cookie sheet for 24 hours. When ready to use, place in 450° oven for 5 minutes, until brown and puffy.

Watch carefully!

Notes

Rustic Cucumber and Tomato Sandwiches with Goat Cheese

- 1 cucumber chopped
- 1 red onion, chopped finely
- 2 medium ripe tomatoes, chopped
- 1 t. dried oregano
- ¼ c. olive oil
- ¼ c. red wine vinegar
- 1 T. honey
- 1 8 oz. pkg. cream cheese (softened)
- butter
- 4 oz. goat cheese crumbled
- 1 c. Italian bread crumbs
- salt and pepper
- 8 grain bread or bread of choice

In a large bowl combine cucumbers, onion, tomatoes, oregano, goat cheese and Italian bread crumbs; add salt and pepper to taste; Set aside. Whisk together olive oil, vinegar, and honey. Add 4 T. of this mixture to cucumber mix. Set aside. Mix the remaining oil mixture into 1 8oz. pkg of cream cheese.

To make the sandwiches, butter slices of 8 grain bread. Spread cream cheese mixture on top of butter. Refrigerate bread slices for 1 hour until

Notes

Rustic Cucumber and Tomato Sandwiches
with Goat Cheese Continued

firm. Trim crusts. Cut each slice into thirds.
Spoon a little cucumber mixture on top of
cream cheese mixture. Sprinkle black pepper on
top.

This is an open-faced sandwich.

Notes

Olive Pecan Savory

- 1 8oz pkg cream cheese softened
- ½ c. sour cream
- ½ c. chopped pecans
- 1 c. chopped green olives
- ¼ t. pepper
- Rye/sourdough/white bread

Beat cream cheese until smooth. Add sour cream. Stir in pecans, green olives, pepper. Butter bread. Spread on cream cheese mixture. Garnish with a slice of olive. This works well as an open faced sandwich, but for a different look, you could use 2 slices of bread and have a closed sandwich. The dark rye bread makes a nice contrast with the white spread.

Notes

Greek Olive Savory

- 1 small can black olives, chopped
- 1 8 oz pkg. mozzarella cheese
- ½ c. Miracle Whip
- 1 stick butter
- 3 green onions, chopped
- 1 clove freshly minced garlic
- cocktail bread slices or baguette

Combine all ingredients and spread on small cocktail bread slices. Bake at 350° until bubbly. Serve warm.

Enjoy!

Notes

Bacon Tomato Cups

- 8 slices of bacon, crisply cooked
- 1 t. basil
- 3 oz. Monterey Jack cheese – grated
- 1 medium tomato, seeded
- ½ small onion
- 1 can flaky biscuits or phyllo dough, cut into small squares

Preheat oven to 375°. Chop bacon, tomato, and onion, grate cheese. Mix all except biscuits/phyllo dough. Separate biscuits into 3 thinner ones. Press into mini muffin pans, fill with bacon mix. (Or press phyllo dough squares into mini muffin pans). Bake 10-12 minutes or until done.

Notes

Mandarin Chicken Sandwich

- 2 c. of cooked chicken
- 1 green onion chopped
- 1 T. toasted sliced almonds
- 1 small can mandarin oranges
- ¼ c. Jarlsberg cheese
- ¼. c. mild cheddar
- mayonnaise

Mix together first 6 ingredients. Add just enough mayonnaise to bind the mixture together. Spread butter on bread. Add filling and top with second slice. Cut into desired shapes. Sprinkle parsley on sides of sandwiches for decoration if desired.

Notes

Smoked Almond Chicken Salad

- 2 c. cooked chicken-pulse in food processor or chop finely
- 3 T. green onions, sliced thinly
- ¼ c. smoked almonds-chopped
- salt to taste
- mayonnaise
- butter
- bread
- parsley for decoration – if desired

Mix together first 4 ingredients. Add just enough mayonnaise to bind the mixture together. Spread butter on bread. Add filling and top with second slice. Cut into desired shapes. Sprinkle parsley on sides of sandwiches for decoration if desired.

Notes

Jarlsberg Chicken Salad – Amy's Favorite

- 2 c. cooked chicken-pulse in food processor or chop finely
- 3 T. green onions, sliced thinly
- ¼-½ c. Jarlsberg cheese-shredded (from the Newcastle Cheese Shop of course!)
- salt and pepper to taste
- mayonnaise
- butter
- bread
- parsley for decoration – if desired

Mix together first 4 ingredients. Add just enough mayonnaise to bind the mixture together. Spread butter on bread. Add filling and top with second slice. Cut into desired shapes. Sprinkle parsley on sides of sandwiches for decoration if desired.

Notes

Balsamic Barbecue Chicken Sandwiches

- 2 c. cooked chicken
- 3-4 T. green onions, sliced
- ¼ c. sharp cheddar cheese (grated)
- salt and pepper to taste
- mayonnaise
- butter
- bread
- Balsamic Barbecue Sauce (recipe follows – there will be extra left over)

Mix together first 4 ingredients. Add just enough mayonnaise to bind the mixture together. Spread butter on bread. Spread a thin layer of barbecue sauce on top. Add filling and top with second slice. Cut into desired shapes.

Notes

Balsamic Barbecue Sauce

- 1 c. ketchup
- ¾ c. balsamic vinegar
- ⅓ c. packed brown sugar
- ¼ c. molasses
- 1 T. Worcestershire
- 1 minced garlic clove
- 1 t. dry mustard
- 1 t. ground ginger
- ½ t. salt
- ¼ t. pepper

Combine all ingredients and simmer uncovered, over medium-low heat, stirring occasionally, until mixture is reduced to about 2 cups – 12-15 minutes. Makes 2 cups.

Notes

Spinach Olive Ranch Sandwich

- 1 8oz pkg. cream cheese softened
- ½ c. sour cream
- 1 c. chopped green olives
- ¼ t. pepper
- 1 pkg. ranch dressing mix
- dark rye
- spinach leaves
- butter

Beat cream cheese until smooth. Add sour cream and ranch dressing. Stir in green olives and pepper. Butter 2 slices bread. Spread cream cheese mixture on both slices. Layer fresh spinach leaves on one slice of bread. Close sandwich. Chill before cutting.

Notes

Ham Salad with Homemade Apricot Preserves

- 1 8oz pkg. cream cheese softened
- ½ c. sour cream
- 1 c. black forest ham
- 2 green onions chopped
- dark rye
- butter
- homemade apricot preserves (recipe follows) or store-bought apricot preserves

Beat cream cheese until smooth. Add sour cream. Stir in ham and green onions. Using a biscuit cutter or glass, cut bread into circles. Butter each circle. Spread cream cheese ham mixture on top. Place a spoonful of preserves on top. Serve immediately.

Notes

Connie's Homemade Apricot Preserves

- 3 c. fresh apricots – very finely chopped in food processor and leave skins on
- ¼ c. water
- 6 level cups of sugar
- 2 pouches of Certo liquid fruit pectin

Wash apricots do not peel. Pulse in food processor. Jam should have bits of fruit. Measure exact amount of chopped fruit into a large bowl. Add exact amount of sugar and water. Stir mixture occasionally and let stand for 10 minutes. Add in Certo and stir until sugar is dissolved. Stir constantly for about 3 minutes until mixture is no longer grainy. A few sugar crystals may remain. Pour into containers and cover. Disposable plastic containers work well. Let sit on counter for 24 hours. Store in freezer for up to one year or you can refrigerate for 3 weeks. Makes about 7 cups.

Notes

Roasted Garlic and Herb Cucumber Sandwiches

- 8 cloves garlic
- 2 T. fresh basil, chopped
- ½ t. dried thyme
- ⅔ c. cream cheese – softened
- ¼ c. mayonnaise or sour cream
- 2 T. fresh chives, chopped
- ⅛ t. salt
- Pepper
- butter
- bread rounds (use any kind of bread you would like, we especially like to use dill bread or buttermilk bread, cut the bread into round circles, or interesting shapes)

Wrap garlic cloves in foil. Bake at 500° for 30 minutes. Squeeze cloves to extract garlic pulp. Discard skins.

With food processor on, drop garlic, basil, and thyme through food chute; process until minced. Add cream cheese and remaining ingredients; process until smooth.

Butter bread slices, spoon a small amount of the roasted garlic mixture on a bread slice. Top with a cucumber slice. Sprinkle with a little black pepper. Makes about 1 cup of spread.

Notes

Desserts

Lazy Peach Pie

- 1 lg can peaches
- ½ c. butter
- 1 c. sugar
- 1 c. flour
- ½ t. salt
- ¾ c. milk
- 2 t. baking powder

Melt butter in a 9x13 inch pan while preheating oven to 350°. Sift sugar, flour and salt in bowl. Mix in milk. Pour batter into butter. Add peaches. Do Not Mix! Sprinkle with cinnamon and sugar.

Bake at 350° for 1 hour until brown and is set.

Notes

Pecan Pie Bars

Crust

- ⅔ c. sugar
- ½ c. butter-softened
- 1 t. vanilla
- 1 ½ c. flour

Filling

- ⅔ c. packed brown sugar
- ½ c. corn syrup
- 1 t. vanilla
- ¼ t. salt
- 3 eggs
- 1 c. chopped pecans

Semisweet chocolate chips, melted Heat oven to 350°. Lightly grease bottom and sides of 9x13 inch pan. In large bowl, mix sugar, butter and vanilla. Stir in flour; mix well. Press dough in bottom and ½ up sides of pan. Bake 15-17 minutes or until edges are light brown. Beat brown sugar, corn syrup, vanilla, salt and eggs with spoon. Stir in pecans. Pour over crust.

Notes

Pecan Pie Bars Continued

Bake 25-30 minutes or until set. Loosen edges
from sides of pan while warm; cool completely.
For bars, cut into 9 rows by 4 rows. Dip 1 end
of each bar into melted chocolate. Lay flat to
dry. Makes about 36 bars.

Notes

Rum Balls

- 1 c. cookie crumbs
- 1 c. powdered sugar
- 1½ c. finely chopped walnuts
- 2 T. light corn syrup
- 4 T. rum
- 2 T. cocoa

Combine all ingredients except nuts. Mix well. Form into 1 inch balls. Roll each in walnuts. Air dry 1 hour. Makes 36 balls, will keep for 2 weeks.

Notes

Limoncello and Dried Cherry Bread Pudding

- 1 large loaf of French bread
- ⅔ c. dried sweet cherries
- 4 eggs
- ½ c. sugar
- 2 c. milk
- ½ c. limoncello liqueur
- 2½ c. whipping cream
- 1 t. vanilla

Preheat oven to 325°. Tear bread into small pieces and place in a large, round greased baking dish, layering the bread with dried cherries. Beat together the eggs, sugar, milk, limoncello, cream and vanilla, and pour over the bread and cherries. Let stand for 1 hour. Bake in a 325° oven for 50-60 minutes, or until lightly browned and the tip of a knife when inserted comes out clean. If desired, top with a little whipped cream mixed with 2 T. limoncello. Makes 6-8 servings.

Notes

Strawberry Shortcake

- 6 c. sliced strawberries
- ½ c sugar
- 2 c. flour
- 2 t. baking powder
- ¼ t. salt
- ½ c. butter
- 1 beaten egg
- ¾ c. buttermilk
- 1 c. whipping cream, whipped

In a small bowl stir together strawberries and ¼ c. sugar. Set aside. Stir together the remaining sugar, flour, baking powder and salt. Cut in the butter until mixture resembles coarse crumbs. Combine the egg and milk; add to dry mixture. Stir just to moisten. Spread the batter into a greased 8x1½ inch round cake pan.

Bake in a 450° oven for 15-18 minutes or until a toothpick inserted in center comes out clean. Cool in pan for 10 minutes. Remove from pan. Split into 2 layers. Spoon half of the berries and whipped cream over the first layer. Top with second layer, remaining strawberries and whipped cream. Serve immediately. Makes about 8 servings.

Notes

Chocolate Almond Macaroon Tea Bars

- 2 c. chocolate graham crackers, crushed
- 6 T. butter, melted
- 6 T. powdered sugar
- 1 can sweetened condensed milk
- 3¾ c. coconut
- 1 c. sliced almonds toasted
- 1 c. semi sweet chocolate chips
- ¼ c. whipping cream

Preheat oven to 350°. Grease a 9x13 inch baking dish. Combine graham cracker crumbs, melted butter and powdered sugar in a large bowl. Firmly press crumb mixture on the bottom of prepared pan. Stir together sweetened condensed milk, coconut, and almonds in a large bowl mixing well. Carefully drop mixture by spoonfuls over crust and spread evenly. Bake 20-25 minutes or until coconut edges just begin to brown. Cool. Place chocolate chips and whipping cream in a medium microwave safe bowl. Microwave on high for 1 minute and stir. If necessary microwave on high for an additional 10 seconds at a time stirring after each heating until chips are melted and mixture is smooth

Notes

Chocolate Almond Macaroon Tea Bars Continued

when stirred. Cool until slightly thickened. Spread over cooled bars. Cover; refrigerate several hours or until thoroughly chilled. Cut into bars. Makes about 36 bars.

Notes

Chocolate Cheese Cake

- 1 ¾ c. chocolate graham cracker crumbs
- ½ c. butter, melted
- 3 T. granulated sugar
- 2 squares (1 oz. each) unsweetened baking chocolate
- ¼ c. butter
- ¾ c. sugar
- 1 3oz pkg. cream cheese softened
- 1 t. milk
- 2 c. whipping cream

- Additional whipping cream – which has been beat into stiff peaks for decorative topping
- Cocoa powder

Mix graham cracker crumbs, ½ c. melted butter and 3 T. sugar in small bowl. Press into the bottom of a 8x8 inch square pan.

Place baking chocolate in a small microwave-safe bowl. Microwave on high 1-1½ minute or until chocolate is melted and smooth when stirred. Beat butter, sugar, cream cheese and milk in medium bowl until well blended and smooth; fold in melted chocolate.

Notes

Chocolate Cheese Cake Continued

Beat 2 c. whipping cream until stiff peaks form. Fold into chocolate mixture and spoon onto crust. Cover, refrigerate until firm about 3 hours. For a special tea party, cut into 1 inch squares. Place each square into small glass condiment cups or use small baking/candy cups. Using the extra whipping cream, pipe a dollop of cream onto each square. Dust with cocoa powder if desired.

Notes

Peppermint Candy Shortbread

Shortbread Cookie

- 1 c. butter, softened
- ⅓ c. sugar
- 2½ c. all purpose flour

Coating

- 8 oz. white chocolate chips
- ⅔ c. crushed hard peppermint candy (candy canes work very well)

Beat butter until creamy; gradually add sugar, beating well. Add flour, beating just until blended.

Divide dough into 3 equal portions. Place a portion of dough on an ungreased cookie sheet; roll into a 6 inch circle. Score partly through the dough into 8 triangles. Repeat with other two portions.

Bake at 325° for 25 minutes or until barely golden. Cool on cookie sheets for 5 minutes. Remove and let cook completely on wire racks. Working very carefully, separate disks into

Notes

Peppermint Candy
Shortbread Continued

wedges. Shortbread is very fragile.

Melt vanilla chips in microwave for 30 seconds on half power or until completely melted. Carefully dip wide edges of shortbread in coating. Place on wax paper.

Immediately sprinkle crushed candy over coated edges. Let set until chocolate is hardened.

Notes

Pumpkin Bars

- 4 eggs
- 1⅔ c. granulated sugar
- 1 c. oil
- 1 (16 oz) can pumpkin
- 2 c. flour
- 2 t. cinnamon
- 2 t. baking powder
- 1 t. salt
- 1 t. soda

Frosting

- 1 (3 oz) pkg. cream cheese
- ½ c. butter, softened
- 1 t. vanilla
- 2 c. powdered sugar

Beat together eggs, granulated sugar, oil and pumpkin until light. Stir in sifted dry ingredients. Mix thoroughly. Spread into an ungreased jelly roll pan. Bake at 350° for 25-30 minutes. Let cool; frost. Cut into squares.

Frosting: Cream the cream cheese until soft and smooth. Add softened butter. Stir in vanilla and powdered sugar. Beat well.

Notes

Homemade Chocolate Pudding

- 3 c. milk
- ¼ c. sugar – if you like it a bit sweeter add more sugar
- ½ t. vanilla
- ⅔ c. chocolate chips
- ⅛ t. salt
- ¼ c. cornstarch

Mix 2 cups of the milk, the sugar, salt and chocolate chips in microwave safe bowl. Microwave on high for 3-7 minutes until melted. Whisk mixture until chocolate is thoroughly mixed. Mix remaining milk and cornstarch and stir it into hot chocolate mixture. Microwave for 2 more minutes, then stir, and microwave 1 minute more, or until mixture thickens. Stir in vanilla and serve.

Notes

Apricot Bars

- ⅔ c. dried apricots, chopped
- ½ c. butter
- ¼ c. granulated sugar
- 1⅓ c. flour
- 2 eggs
- 1 c. brown sugar packed
- ½ t. baking powder
- ¼ t. salt
- ½ t. vanilla
- ½ c. chopped nuts
- ½ c. shredded coconut

Preheat oven to 350°. Combine butter, granulated sugar and 1 cup flour, and blend together until crumbly. Press into bottom of greased 8x8 inch square pan. Bake about 15-18 minutes, until lightly browned. Beat eggs, vanilla and gradually beat in brown sugar. Sift remaining ⅓ c. flour with baking powder and salt. Blend into egg mixture. Stir in nuts, coconut and apricots. Spread over baked layer. Bake for about 30 minutes longer. Cool. Cut into bars. Makes about 16 bars.

Notes

Summer Fruit Heaven Pie

Pie

- 12 oz cream cheese softened
- ½ c. sugar
- ½ pint whipping cream
- Fresh strawberries

Blueberry Glaze

- 1 pkg. frozen or fresh blueberries
- ⅓ c. sugar

Pie:

Using an electric mixer, mix the softened cream cheese and sugar until mixed. In another bowl, whip the cream until stiff peaks form. Gently fold the cream into the cream cheese; blend well. Slice the strawberries in half and place on the bottom and sides of a 9 inch deep-dish pie plate. Pour cream cheese mixture over top and chill until firm. Make the blueberry glaze while mixture is chilling.

Blueberry Glaze:

Notes

Summer Fruit Heaven Pie
Continued

Combine blueberries and sugar in a saucepan and cook over low heat until thickened. Be care not to break up the berries too much. Cool to room temperature. Spoon over cheese mixture and and chill several hours or overnight.

The glaze won't be real thick and it goes down into the cream cheese mixture.

Notes

Peppermint Brittle

- 1½ c. flour
- ½ t. baking soda
- ¼ t. salt
- ¾ c. unsalted butter – melted and cooled slightly
- ½ c. sugar
- ⅓ c. brown sugar
- 1 t. vanilla
- 10 oz. white chocolate chips
- 1-3 t. oil to thin white chocolate
- ¾ c. candy canes crushed (put them in a zip-lock bag and crush them with a hammer)

Preheat oven to 350°. Line a 9x13 inch pan with parchment paper. Stir flour, baking soda and salt in a medium bowl. In a large bowl stir in melted butter, both sugars and vanilla until smooth. Stir in flour mixture until just blended. Stir in 1 c. of white chocolate chips and ½ c. crushed candy canes. Press dough onto the parchment paper in 9x13 inch pan. Bake cookie until top is firm and dark golden, about 30 minutes. Be sure they are baked long enough so they will be brittle when cool. Transfer to rack and cool.

Notes

Peppermint Brittle
Continued

In a small bowl melt white chocolate chips with 1 t. oil in microwave on half power for about 30 seconds. Stir add 1-2 t. more oil if needed to thin to make a drizzle consistency. Melt 30 sec. more until chips are melted.

Drizzle half of the melted chocolate in thin lines over pan. Sprinkle remaining crushed candy canes over chocolate. Drizzle more white chocolate over top. Let stand until chocolate sets about 1 hour. Break into irregular shapes about 2-3 inches pieces or cut into bars. Store in an airtight container at room temperature. Makes about 24 pieces.

Notes

Cranberry Ginger Chocolate Cups

- 1 3 oz pkg cream cheese softened
- 1 t. vanilla
- 3¼ c. powdered sugar
- 1 c. dried cranberries
- ½ c. coarsely chopped sliced almonds
- 4 t. finely chopped crystallized ginger (use food processor to chop)
- 1 12 oz. pkg semisweet chocolate chips
- 1 T. shortening
- Sliced almonds to decorate top

In large mixing bowl, beat cream cheese and vanilla with electric mixer for 30 seconds, using medium speed (a stand mixer works extremely well). Slowly beat in powdered sugar until combined (mixture will be dry). Stir in cranberries, almonds and ginger. Knead mixture in bowl until it holds together. Shape into 1 inch balls (a small ice-cream scoop/or round teaspoon works great to form the balls.) Place balls in small foil or paper candy cups.

In a saucepan combine chocolate and shortening. Stir over low heat until melted. Spoon melted chocolate over the candies. Top each one with an almond slice. Let stand until set – about 1 hour. Store in refrigerator.

Notes

Laura's Best of Show Cookies

- ½ c. butter
- ½ c. brown sugar
- ½ t. vanilla
- 1 c. flour
- ¼ t. salt
- 1 c. finely chopped walnuts
- jam or preserves (homemade is the best!)

Mix all ingredients together except jam/preserves. Form into 1 inch balls and bake at 350° for about 10-12 minutes. Take out of oven. While still warm, lightly press a spoon into the cookie to make an indentation. Let cool completely. Spoon jam/preserves into center of cookie.

Enjoy!

Notes

Ginger Cookies

- ¾ c. shortening
- 1 c. sugar
- ¼ c. molasses
- 1 egg
- 2 c. flour (less 2 T.)
- ¼ t. salt
- 2 t. cinnamon
- 1 t. cloves
- 1 t. ginger
- 2 t. baking soda
- extra sugar for rolling

Cream sugar and shortening, beat in molasses, then egg. Mix dry ingredients together. Add to creamed mixture. Form into a ball which is about 1 teaspoon of dough and roll in sugar. Do not flatten. Bake at 350° for 10 minutes or until done.

Notes

Toffee Tea Bar Cookies

- ¾ c. butter, melted
- 1¾ c. vanilla wafer crumbs
- 6 T. cocoa
- ¼ c. sugar
- 1 can sweetened condensed milk
- 1 c. semi sweet chocolate chips
- ¾ c. SKOR English Toffee Bits
- 1 c. chopped walnuts

Preheat oven to 350°. Mix melted butter, crumbs, cocoa and sugar in a medium bowl. Press into the bottom of a 9x13 inch pan. Pour sweetened condensed milk evenly over the top of crumb mixture. Top with chocolate chips and toffee bits, then nuts. Press down firmly. Bake 25-30 minutes or until lightly browned. Cool completely in pan. Cut into bars. Store covered at room temperature. Makes about 36 bars.

Notes

Double Chocolate Chip Cookies

- 1 c. butter softened
- 1 c. granulated sugar
- ¾ c. packed brown sugar
- 2 t. vanilla
- ½ t. salt
- 2 eggs
- 2 c. flour
- ½ c. cocoa
- 1 t. baking soda
- 2 c. chocolate chips

Preheat oven to 375°. Beat butter, sugars, vanilla and salt in a large bowl until creamy. Add eggs; beat well. In a separate bowl stir together flour, cocoa, baking soda and chocolate chips. Add to creamed mixture and beat until well blended. Drop by teaspoons onto an ungreased cookie sheet. Bake 8-10 minutes until set. Cool on wire rack. Makes about 5 dozen cookies.

Notes

Orange Cranberry Oatmeal Cookies

- 1 c. butter, softened
- 1 c. brown sugar, packed
- ½ c. granulated sugar
- 2 eggs
- 1 t. vanilla
- 1 t. orange extract
- 1½ c. flour
- 1 t. baking soda
- ½ t. salt
- 2 c. quick oats
- 1 c. old fashioned oats (or you can use 3 c. quick oats)
- 1 c. cranberries
- 1 c. walnuts, chopped

Preheat oven to 350°. In a large bowl beat together butter and sugars until creamy. Add eggs, vanilla, and orange extract, beat well. Combine flour, baking soda and salt in a separate bowl. Mix into creamed mixture. Stir in oats, cranberries and walnuts. Drop by rounded teaspoons onto ungreased cookie sheet. Bake 8-10 minutes for chewy or 10-12 minutes for crisp. Cool 1 minute on cookie sheet, remove to wire rack. Makes about 4 dozen cookies.

Notes

Espresso Tea Cookies

Frosting

- 1 c. brown sugar packed
- ¼ c. butter
- ¼ c. light cream
- 1 ⅓ c. sifted powdered sugar

Cookies

- 2¼ c. flour
- 3 T. instant coffee
- 2 t. ground ginger
- 1 t. baking soda
- 1 t. cinnamon
- ½ t. ground cloves
- ¾ c. butter, softened
- ½ c. granulated sugar
- ½ c. packed light brown sugar
- 1 egg
- ¼ c. molasses
- 2-3 T. turbinado sugar

Frosting:

In a heavy saucepan combine brown sugar, butter, and cream. Cook and stir over medium heat to a full boil; boil 1 minute, stirring

Notes

Espresso Tea Cookies
Continued

constantly. Remove from heat. Whisk in powdered sugar until smooth. Let cool about 30 minutes. Whisk occasionally.

Cookies:

In a medium bowl, combine flour, coffee, ginger, baking soda, cinnamon and cloves. Set aside.

In a large bowl, beat butter with an electric mixer on medium speed for 30 seconds. Gradually add the granulated sugar and brown sugar, beating on low speed until combined. Beat in the egg and molasses until combined. Beat in as much of the flour mixture as you can with the mixer. Stir in any remaining flour mixture. Cover and chill dough for 2 hours or until easy to handle. Shape dough into balls (about 1 T. dough each). Roll balls in the turbinado sugar. Place about 2½ inches apart on an ungreased cookie sheet. Flatten balls slightly. Bake in a 350° oven for 12-15 minutes or until edges are set. Let stand on cookie sheet for 2

Notes

Espresso Tea Cookies
Continued

minutes. Transfer to wire racks and cool. Frost bottoms of half the cookies with a generous 1 T. brown sugar frosting each. Place remaining cookies atop the iced cookies to create sandwiches. Makes 12 sandwich cookies.

Notes

Apricot Almond Tea Cookies

- 1 c. flour
- 1 t. baking soda
- 1 c. butter
- ¾ c. packed brown sugar
- ½ c. granulated sugar
- 1 egg
- 1 T. amaretto liqueur or use almond extract to taste
- 2½ c. quick cooking oats
- 1 c. dried apricots
- ¼ t. salt
- ½ c. finely chopped almonds
- 2 c. powdered sugar
- 3 T. amaretto liqueur

Preheat over to 375°. In a large bowl beat the butter until softened. Add the brown sugar and sugar and beat until fluffy. Add egg and 1 T. amaretto and mix well. Stir together the flour, baking soda and salt. Add to the butter mixture and beat until well mixed. Stir in the oats, apricots, and almonds. Drop by rounded teaspoons onto an ungreased cookie sheet and bake for about 8-10 minutes or until set. Cool on cookie sheet for about 1 minute, before

Notes

Apricot Almond Tea Cookies
Continued

removing.

Stir together powdered sugar and enough of the 2-3 T. amaretto to make an icing of drizzling consistency. Drizzle over the cookies.

Notes

Scones

Tips on Making Scones

Use quality ingredients.

Use cold butter, don't let it soften – cold butter makes the scones rise higher.

Drain fruit very well.

Add fruit just before the buttermilk and barely mix it into flour mixture.

Add only enough buttermilk to make dough stick together.

If dough is too sticky when you pat it on the floured board, add more flour.

If dough is too dry and crumbles when you try and pat it on the floured board, add more buttermilk.

If you are using frozen fruit, make sure it does not thaw out. Mix it in quickly and cut scones fast. If it thaws out, the dough becomes very sticky and is a mess!

Make sure oven is hot and preheated to 400°.

Bake until nicely browned. Oven times vary widely. Use your best judgment.

Blueberry Peach Scones

- 3 c. self-rising flour
- ¾ c. granulated sugar
- 1 stick butter
- ¾ c. buttermilk
- ½ c. fresh peaches sliced
- ½ c. fresh blueberries

Mix together flour and sugar. Use pastry cutter to cut in butter. Mixture should resemble coarse cornmeal. Add blueberries and peaches. Add buttermilk and stir. Turn out on a floured board. Pat out to 1 inch thick. Cut with a small biscuit cutter or into triangles. Bake in preheated 400° oven for 12-20 minutes or until nicely browned and done – depending on your oven. Cool in pan. Glaze with a mixture of powdered sugar, milk and vanilla. Scones can be stored in a sealed container and reheated in foil. Makes about 16 scones.

Enjoy!

Notes

Cinnamon Apple Pecan Scones

- 3 c. self-rising flour
- ¾ c. granulated sugar
- 1 stick of butter
- ¾ to 1 c. buttermilk
- ¼ c. applesauce
- ½ c. chopped apples

Topping

- ½ c. oatmeal
- ¼ c. butter
- ¼ c. brown sugar
- ¼ c. pecans – chopped and toasted

Mix together flour and sugar. Use pastry cutter to cut in butter. Mixture should resemble coarse cornmeal. Add applesauce and chopped apples. Add ¾ c. buttermilk and stir. Turn out on a floured board. Pat into a large circle about 1 inch thick. In a small bowl combine topping ingredients. Add enough topping to cover circle. Press topping into scone dough. Cut with a small biscuit cutter. Bake in preheated 400° oven for 12-20 minutes or until nicely browned and done – depending on your oven. Cool in pan. Glaze with a mixture of powdered sugar, milk and vanilla. Can be stored in a sealed container and reheated in foil. Makes about 16 scones

Notes

Jamaican Banana Scones

- 3 c. self-rising flour
- ½ c. granulated sugar
- 1 stick of unsalted butter
- ½ c. mashed bananas
- ¾ to 1 c. buttermilk

Glaze

- ¼ c. toasted pecans
- ⅛ c. sweetened coconut
- ½ c. packed brown sugar
- 4 t. butter
- 4 t. lime juice
- 4 t. rum or ⅛ t. rum extract

Mix together flour and sugar. Use pastry cutter to cut in butter. Mixture should resemble coarse cornmeal. Add mashed bananas. Add ¾ cup of buttermilk and stir. If mixture is too dry add a little more buttermilk. Turn out on a floured board. Pat out to 1 inch thick. Cut with a small biscuit cutter or into triangles. Bake in preheated 400° oven for 12-20 minutes or until nicely browned and done – depending on your oven. Brush with Lime Glaze. Scones can be stored in a sealed container and reheated in foil.

Notes

Jamaican Banana Scones
Continued

Makes about 16 scones.

Lime Glaze:

Melt butter in microwave or on stove. Stir in coconut, brown sugar, lime juice, and rum. Brush glaze over warm scones. Sprinkle with toasted pecans.

Enjoy!

Notes

Anniversary Scones

- 3 c. self-rising flour
- ½ c. granulated sugar
- 1 stick of unsalted butter
- ¾ to 1 c. buttermilk
- ½ c. raspberries
- ½ c. white chocolate chips
- ½ c. coconut

Mix together flour and sugar. Use pastry cutter to cut in butter. Mixture should resemble coarse cornmeal. Add raspberries, chips and coconut. Add buttermilk and stir. If mixture is too dry, add a little more buttermilk. Turn out on a floured board. Pat out to 1 inch thick. Cut with a small biscuit cutter or into triangles. Bake in preheated 400° oven for 12-20 minutes or until nicely browned and done – depending on your oven. Glaze with a mixture of powdered sugar, milk and vanilla. Scones can be stored in a sealed container and reheated in foil. Makes about 16 scones.

Notes

Mango Pineapple Scones

- 3 c. self-rising flour
- ½ c. granulated sugar
- 1 stick of unsalted butter
- ½ to ¾ c. buttermilk
- ½ c. chopped mangoes (dried or fresh)
- ¼ c. chopped pineapple (use food processor and pule lightly, save the juice)
- ½ c. coconut

Mix together flour and sugar. Use pastry cutter to cut in butter. Mixture should resemble coarse cornmeal. If you are using dried mangoes you will need to reconstitute them. To do this, drain the pineapple juice from the can into a microwave safe bowl. Heat in the microwave and add to the dried mangoes. Let them sit for about 10 minutes. Drain, but save the juice. Add mangoes, pineapple and coconut to the flour/sugar mixture. Add ¼ c. of the pineapple juice, add ½ c. of buttermilk and stir. If mixture is too dry, add a little more buttermilk. Turn out on a floured board. Pat out to 1 inch thick. Cut with a small biscuit cutter or into triangles. Bake in preheated 400° oven for 12-20 minutes or until nicely browned and done – depending

Notes

Mango Pineapple Scones
Continued

on your oven. Glaze with a mixture of powdered sugar, milk and vanilla. Scones can be stored in a sealed container and reheated in foil. Makes about 16 scones.

Notes

Index

Index Continued

Index Continued

About the Author

Amy Lawrence began her tea room in August of 2003. Previously she had been a special education teacher for 11 years teaching learning disabled and autistic students. She took a two year break to be home with her two sons. In August of 2002 while having tea with my mother, she said, "This is what I want to do now! I want my own tea room. I love to cook and have always enjoyed catering for special parties." In November of 2002, she attended a tea conference and also became a certified tea consultant. It all began from there. With the help of dedicated family and friends, she finally opened her tea room on August 27, 2003. In July 2006, Tea Experience Digest named An Afternoon to Remember Tea Parlor and Gifts the Reader's Choice Award for Best Small City Tea Room in the U.S. At the present time, Amy has self-published 4 cookbooks and is currently working on a new book on afternoon teas.

www.ingramcontent.com/pod-product-compliance
Lightning Source LLC
LaVergne TN
LVHW011240080426
835509LV00005B/575

My Jamaican Father

Father

JULIE WOOD